KNIT YOUR GARDEN

Creative Pouches and Vegetables Based on the Natural World

YUN JEONG

Knit Your Garden
CREATIVE POUCHES AND VEGETABLES BASED ON THE NATURAL WORLD

Photography by Jennifer Lim

iUniverse books may be ordered through booksellers or by contacting:

iUniverse
1663 Liberty Drive
Bloomington, IN 47403
www.iuniverse.com
844-349-9409

ISBN: 978-1-6632-3191-8 (sc)
ISBN: 978-1-6632-3192-5 (e)

Library of Congress Control Number: 2022913469

Print information available on the last page.

iUniverse rev. date: 03/30/2023

Contents

Special thanks to

MY MOTHER, CHARLES, HANYU AND FAMILY

GREETING

I have fond childhood memories of my mother knitting sweaters for me.

I'm not sure exactly when I started knitting. As I learned to knit, I wanted to infuse my own ideas with the love and care that I had received. I'm forever grateful for my artistic family, who inspired and nurtured my knitting journey.

I started knitting actively when I was pregnant and living in Toronto.

It was immensely enjoyable to make baby sweaters, socks, and hats in anticipation of my winter baby. The little one is now a creative, meticulously observant seven-year-old. Recently, I taught him how to knit simple garter stitches. We finished a square cup coaster and a hat.

Rhythmic, repetitive knitting can provide a happy mental break from daily challenges for both children and grown-ups alike.

For many years, I had weekly workshops with fellow knitters in Toronto, Canada, until I moved. Many ideas were conceived during this time, and patterns such as children's sweaters, scarves, hats, cardigans, and many bags were born. I still keep in touch with these knitters; we remain good friends. Some of them have become reliable test knitters—they try out different sizes of patterns before I release the patterns to the public. I truly appreciate them for supporting me from afar.

As of this writing, I teach knitting to eight- to nine-year-old children at an elementary school in Vancouver, British Columbia. It is remarkable that I'm learning more from the children, from their fresh perspectives and creativity.

You can find my original knitting patterns on Ravelry (go to ravelry.com, then search for yunique-crafts), and I actively engage with my followers and fellow knitters on Instagram @yunique.crafts.

I hope we will connect soon.

Warm regards,
YUN JEONG

INTRODUCTION

Welcome to My Garden

I find joy in things that grow. Nature grows, whether we notice it or not. My child and I have experienced that there's always something new to find and always something to be thankful for.

This book is designed to be easy to follow for both children and grownups. Each item is designed to be completed in a short time, which is achievable even if you have busy little children around.

I divided the book into two parts. Part I is "Pouches," which can store children's nature treasures or grown-ups' essential belongings.

Once you make the first pouch, it will be more enjoyable to make others.

Part II is "Vegetables." These are perfect "food" toys for children and seasonal decorations. You can use them as garlands, key chains, bag charms, or gift tags.

Knitting in the round uses double-point needles, and natural shapes are created without seams, just as fruits and vegetables are seamless.

The patterns in this book are quite easy, even if you are a beginner. Still, if you would like a helping hand, please refer to the list of abbreviations and the techniques explained in the back of the book.

I hope you find calm joy when knitting them.

The following comment is from one of my Instagram followers, who uses her own IG to show how to spend time with children in a natural way:

I'm a homeschooling mother of three kids, and we always enjoy exploring and putting our hands and feet in nature. What I deeply get excited about Yun's work is how she joins nature and childhood with such warmth and creativity. I love how her designs are simple, balanced, and thoughtful. As a complete beginner, I was able to experience the joy of knitting. And the looks on the kids' faces when they get to see the knitted version of their favorite vegetables. Spread the love, Yun!

—Jeesoo

POUCH PATTERNS

Little hands, little treasures found along the path—acorns and stones, natural objects, familiar but hidden from a grown-up's eyes—are precious in child's eyes.

Dear friend,

I started making this series of knitted pouches for my son to use for the objects he found when we went on our little walks. I wanted them to be easy and quick to knit and simply an enjoyable experience for knitters.

The patterns are ordered by level of difficulty. My hope is that you will enjoy knitting all of them throughout the passing of seasons.

Best of luck,

YUN

PS: These pouches can hold treasures and surprises. You may begin to see the world anew.

Part I includes a provisional cast-on, which holds on to live stitches. This allows you to continue knitting in the opposite direction later on. You will knit in the round using double-point needles. You can enjoy creating natural shapes with simple ways to increase and decrease the size.

WHAT TO USE FOR MAKING POUCHES

Knitting Needles

- 4.0 mm (US6) 12–16" circular needle and set of double-point needles
- 3.25 mm (US3) set of double-point needles
- 4.0 mm (US6) crochet hook

Yarn

- fingering, sport, DK, or worsted weight yarn scraps

You can use any yarn you have on hand; just make sure each is the same weight.

You can hold two strands of different yarn together for variegated-color works. Information on the specific yarn I used is included in each pattern for reference.

Notions

- place marker for marking the beginning of the round when you work in round
- tapestry needle for finishing or weaving in the tails
- cotton stuffing or yarn scraps

HOW TO START KNITTING POUCHES

Stretchy Hem

All the pouches start in the same way, as described below. The number of cast-on stitches will vary. Please refer to the patterns for each, starting cast-on stitch numbers.

3.25 mm (US3) double-point needles (dpns); work in flat

Provisional cast on (CO) with given number of stiches (sts) in each pattern (see "Techniques" on page 115)

R1 (RS): k3, (p1, k1)*, rep* to the last 2 sts, k2

R2 (WS): p3, (k1, p1)*, rep* to the last 2 sts, p2

R3–R14: rep R1–R2

Fold in half; place the loop or string in the fold.

Place 2 needles parallel.

Needle 1: sts from provisional CO

Needle 2: sts on working needle

Next R: k 2 sts together from both needles, as shown in photo

GRAPEFRUIT POUCH

YARN TO USE

The Loop with a Leaf

- fine weight, Berroco Ultra Alpaca, lime, 36 m

Grapefruit

- worsted weight, Lion Brand Vanna's Choice, orange, 50 m

THE LOOP WITH A LEAF

3.25 mm (US3) dpns, green; work in round

CO 3 sts

R1: k3, work as I-cord (see "Techniques" on page 117)

R2: (kfb)*, rep* to BOR [6 sts]

R3: k in round

R4: (k1, M1L, k1, M1R, k1) x 2 [10 sts]

R5: k in round

R6: (k2, M1L, k1, M1R, k2) x 2 [14 sts]

R7: k in round

R8: (k3, M1L, k1, M1R, k3) x 2 [18 sts]

R9: k in round

R10: (k4, M1L, k1, M1R, k4) x 2 [22 sts]

R11: k in round

R12: (k5, M1L, k1, M1R, k5) x 2 [26 sts]

R13: k in round

R14: (k6, M1L, k1, M1R, k6) x 2 [30 sts]

R15: k in round

R16: (k7, M1L, k1, M1R, k7) x 2 [34 sts]

R17: k in round

R18: (k8, M1L, k1, M1R, k8) x 2 [38 sts]

R19: k in round

Place 38 sts onto 2 dpns, 19 sts on each dpn.

R20: (ssk, k to the last 2 sts of the needle, k2tog) x 2

R21: k in round

R22–R35: rep R20–R21

You have 3 sts on each dpn. Place initial 3 sts on pm or any scrap of yarn. Work on I-cord (see "Techniques" on page 117) with next 3 sts, using yarn at the end (stitch 4, 5, 6 from photo).

Work on 3 sts I-cord for 40 -45cm (16-18in).

Join I-cord with sts from pm or yarn scrap, as shown in photo. Now you will have 6 sts on 1 dpn.

Next R: (k2tog) x 3 [3 sts]

Next 5 rows, 3 sts I-cord

Next R: k1, kfb, k1 [4 sts]

Keep working on 4 sts I-cord for 5 cm (2 in) to make a stem.

Cut yarn. Using a tapestry needle, thread through the remaining stitches. Pull tightly.

Stitch 1,2,3 from PM

Stitch 4,5,6 on working needle

Stitch 4,1,5,2,6,3

HOW TO TIE A KNOT WITH A STEM

GRAPEFRUIT BODY

Stretchy Hem (instructions on page 3)

3.25 mm (US3) dpns, orange; work in flat

Provisional CO 37 sts

Change to 4.0 mm (US6) needles; work in flat

R1 (WS): p to EOR [37 sts]

R2 (RS): k1, (M1, k5) x 7, M1, k1 [45 sts]

R3 (WS): p to EOR

R4 (RS): k2, (M1, k6) x 6, M1, k5, M1, k2 [53 sts]

R5 (WS): p to EOR

R6 (RS): k2, (M1, K7) x 7, M1, k2 [61 sts]

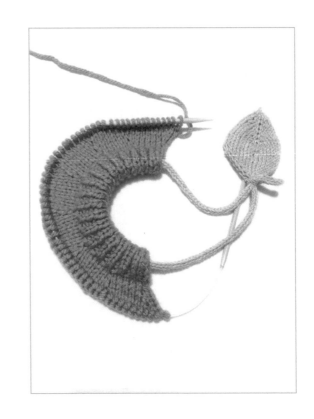

R7 (WS): p to EOR

R8 (RS): k2, (M1, k8) x 7, M1, k3 [69 sts]

R9 (WS): p to EOR

R10 (RS): k to the last 1 st; place pm; join as a round. Move the last 1 st to the left needle.

Work in round from now onward.

R11: k2tog (the last 1 st from R10 and the first stitch from R11), k to BOR [68 sts]

R12–R26: k in round

R27: (k7, k2tog, k6, k2tog) x 4 [60 sts]

R28: k in round

R29: (k6, k2tog, k5, k2tog) x 4 [52 sts]

R30: k in round

R31: (k5, k2tog, k4, k2tog) x 4 [44 sts]

R32: k in round

R33: (k4, k2tog, k3, k2tog) x 4 [36 sts]

R34: (k3, k2tog, k2, k2tog) x 4 [28 sts]

R35: (k2, k2tog, k1, k2tog) x 4 [20 sts]

R36: (k2tog) x 10 [10 sts]

Cut yarn. Using a tapestry needle, thread through the remaining stitches. Pull tightly.

LEMON POUCH

YARN TO USE

The Loop with a Leaf

- fine weight, Berroco Ultra Alpaca, green, 36m

Lemon

- worsted weight, Patons Classic Wool, yellow, 50m

THE LOOP WITH A LEAF

3.25 mm (US3) dpns, green; work in round

CO 3 sts

R1: k3, working as I-cord (see "Techniques" on page 117)

R2: (kfb)*, rep* to BOR [6 sts]

R3: k in round

R4: (k1, M1L, k1, M1R, k1) x 2 [10 sts]

R5–R6: k in round

R7: (k2, M1L, k1, M1R, k2) x 2 [14 sts]

R8–R9: k in round

R10: (k3, M1L, k1, M1R, k3) x 2 [18 sts]

R11–R12: k in round

R13: (k4, M1L, k1, M1R, k4) x 2 [22 sts]

R14–R15: k in round

R16: (k5, M1L, k1, M1R, k5) x 2 [26 sts]

R17–R18: k in round

R19: (k6, M1L, k1, M1R, k6) x 2 [30 sts]

R20–R22: k in round

Place 30 stitches onto 2 double-point needles. You will have 15 stitches on each double-point needle.

R23: (ssk, k to the last 2 sts of the needle, k2tog) x 2

R24: k in round

R25–R33: rep R23–R24 [3 sts on each dpn]

You will have 3 sts on each dpn. Place initial 3 sts on pm or yarn scrap.

Work on I-cord with next 3 sts, using yarn at the end. (See photos from grapefruit instructions.)

Work on 3 sts I-cord for 40-45 cm (16-18 in).

Join I-cord with sts from pm or yarn scrap. Now you will have 6 sts on 1 dpn.

Next R: (k2tog) x 3 [3 sts]

Next 5 rows, 3 sts I-cord

Next R: k1, kfb, k1 [4 sts]

Keep working on 4 sts I-cord for 5 cm (2in) to make a stem.

Cut yarn. Using a tapestry needle, thread through the remaining stitches. Pull tightly.

Tie a knot with the stem, the same as for the grapefruit pouch (page 8).

LEMON BODY

Stretchy Hem (instructions on page 3)

3.25 mm (US3) dpns, yellow; work in flat

Provisional CO 37 sts

Change to 4.0 mm (US6) needles; work in flat

R1(WS): p to EOR [37 sts]

R2(RS): k1, (M1, k5) x 7, M1, k1 [45 sts]

R3(WS): p to EOR

R4(RS): k2, (M1, k8) x 5, M1, k3 [51 sts]

R5(WS): p to EOR

R6(RS): k3, (M1, k9) x 5, M1, k3 [57 sts]

R7(WS): p to EOR

R8(RS): k3, (M1, k10) x 5, M1, k4 [63 sts]

R9(WS): p to EOR

R10(RS): k3, (M1, k11) x 5, M1, k5 [69 sts]

R11(WS): p to EOR

R12(RS): k to EOR

R13(WS): p to EOR

R14(RS): k to the last 1 st; place pm; join as a round. Move the last 1 st to the left needle.

Work in round from now onward.

R15: k2tog (the last 1 st from R14 and the first st from R15), k to BOR [68 sts]

R16: k to the last 1 st; place pm; remove pm from R14

R17: k2tog (the last 1 st from R16 and the first st from R17), k to BOR [67 sts]

R18–R21: k in round

R22: k32, k2tog, k33 [66 sts]

R23–R28: k in round

R29: (k9, k2tog) x 6 [60 sts]

R30: k in round

R31: (k8, k2tog) x 6 [54 sts]

R32: k in round

R33: (k7, k2tog) x 6 [48 sts]

R34: k in round

R35: (k6, k2tog) x 6 [42 sts]

R36: (k5, k2tog) x 6 [36 sts]

R37: (k4, k2tog) x 6 [30 sts]

Change to 3.25 mm (US3) dpns

R38: (CDD) x 10 [10 sts]

R39–R42: k in round

Cut yarn. Using a tapestry needle, thread through the remaining stitches. Pull tightly.

GREEN APPLE POUCH

YARN TO USE

The Loop with a Leaf

- fine weight, Berroco Ultra Alpaca, lime mix, 36m

Green Apple

- sport weight, Premier Yarns Cotton Fair, green, 67m

THE LOOP WITH A LEAF

3.25 mm (US3) dpns, green; work in round

CO 3 sts

R1: k3, working as I-cord (see "Techniques" on page 117)

R2: (kfb)*, rep* to BOR [6 sts]

R3: k in round

R4: (k1, M1L, k1, M1R, k1) x 2 [10 sts]

R5–R6: k in round

R7: (k2, M1L, k1, M1R, k2) x 2 [14 sts]

R8–R9: k in round

R10: (k3, M1L, k1, M1R, k3) x 2 [18 sts]

R11–R12: k in round

R13: (k4, M1L, k1, M1R, k4) x 2 [22 sts]

R14–R15: k in round

R16: (k5, M1L, k1, M1R, k5) x 2 [26 sts]

R17–R18: k in round

R19: (k6, M1L, k1, M1R, k6) x 2 [30 sts]

R20–R22: k in round

Place 30 stitches onto 2 double-point needles. You will have 15 stitches on each double-point needle.

R23: (ssk, k to the last 2 sts of the needle, k2tog) x 2

R24: k in round

R25–R33: rep. R23–R24 [3 sts on each dpn]

You will have 3 sts on each dpn. Place initial 3 sts on pm or yarn scrap.

Work on I-cord with next 3 sts, using yarn at the end. (See photos from grapefruit instructions.)

Work on 3 sts I-cord for 40-45 cm (16-18 in).

Join I-cord with sts from pm or yarn scrap. Now you will have 6 sts on 1 dpn.

Next R: (k2tog) x 3 [3 sts]

Next 5 rows, 3 sts I-cord

Next R: k1, kfb, k1 [4 sts]

Keep working on 4 sts I-cord for 5 cm (2 in) to make a stem.

Cut yarn. Using a tapestry needle, thread through the remaining stitches. Pull tightly.

Tie a knot with the stem, the same as for the grapefruit pouch (page 8).

GREEN APPLE BODY

Stretchy Hem (instructions on page 3)

3.25 mm (US3) dpns, apple green; work in flat

Provisional CO 41 sts

Change to 4.0 mm (US6) needles; work in flat.

R1 (WS): p to EOR [41 sts]

R2 (RS): (k4, M1) x 10, k1 [51 sts]

R3 (WS): p to EOR

R4 (RS): (k5, M1) x 10, k1 [61 sts]

R5 (WS): p to EOR

R6 (RS): (k6, M1) x 10, k1 [71 sts]

R7 (WS): p to EOR

R8 (RS): (k7, M1) x 10, k1 [81 sts]

R9 (WS): p to EOR

R10 (RS): (k8, M1) x 10, k1 [91 sts]

R11 (WS): p to EOR

R12 (RS): k to EOR

R13 (WS): p to EOR

R14(RS): k to the last 1 st. Place pm; join as a round. Move the last 1 st to the left needle.

Work in round from now onward.

R15: k2tog (the last 1 st from R14 and the first st from R15); k to BOR [90 sts]

R16–R21: k in round

R22: (k13, k2tog) x 6 [84 sts]

R23–R24: k in round

R25: (k12, k2tog) x 6 [78 sts]

R26–R27: k in round

R28: (k11, k2tog) x 6 [72 sts]

R29–R30: k in round

R31: (k10, k2tog) x 6 [66 sts]

R32–R33: k in round

R34: (k9, k2tog) x 6 [60 sts]

R35–R36: k in round

R37: (k8, k2tog) x 6 [54 sts]

R38–R42: k in round

R43: (k2tog) x 27 [27 sts]

R44: k in round

R45: (k2tog) x 13, k1 [14 sts]

R46: k in round

R47: (k2tog) x 7 [7 sts]

Place the remaining sts onto pm or yarn scrap. Turn apple inside (WS) out. Place the sts back to dpns from pm or yarn scrap, as shown in photo instructions below.

R48: (k2tog) x 3, k1 [4 sts]

R49: k2, k2tog [3 sts]

Work on I-cord for 15 rows.

Cut yarn. Using a tapestry needle, thread through the remaining stitches. Pull tightly.

With I-cord, tie a knot, as shown in photo instructions below.

BROCCOLI POUCH

YARN TO USE

Broccoli Crown

- DK weight, Jamieson & Smith Shetland 2-ply, 1282 mix and 29 mix, held together, 30m

Broccoli Stalk

- sport weight, Sugar Bush Bliss, mint, 27m

THE STRING WITH A MINI BROCCOLI

3.25 mm (US3) dpns, dark green; work in round

Broccoli Crown

CO 4 sts, with long tail about 20 cm (8 in) to shape the crown at the end.

R1: (pfkb) x 4 [8 sts]

R2: (k1, p1)*, rep* to BOR

R3: (pfkb) x 8 [16 sts]

R4: (k1, p1)*, rep* to BOR

R5: (pfkb, k1, p1, pfkb, p1, k1) x 2, pfkb, k1, p1, k1 [21 sts]

R6: (k1, p1)*, rep* to the last 1 st, k1

R7: (p1, k1)*, rep* to the last 1 st, p1

R8–R9: rep. R6–R7

R10: k1, k2tog, p1, k1, p1, k1, p1, k2tog, k1, p1, k1, p1, k1, k2tog, p1, k1, p1, k1

Connect light green.

R11: [(with dark green) k2, (with light green) k1]*, rep* to BOR

R12: [(with dark green) k2tog, (with light green) k1]*, rep* to BOR [12 sts]

Cut dark green yarn; work with light green yarn only from now onward.

R13: (k2tog)*, rep* to BOR [6 sts]

R14: k in round

BROCCOLI STALK

You will have 3 sts on each dpn. Place initial 3 sts on pm or yarn scrap.

Work on I-cord with next 3 sts using yarn at the end. (Photo instructions from grapefruit on page 7)

Work on 3 sts I-cord for 40-45 cm (16-18 in).

Join I-cord with sts from pm or yarn scrap. Now you will have 6 sts on 1 dpn.

Next R: (k2tog) x 3 [3 sts]

Next 5 rows: 3 sts I-cord

Next R: k1, kfb, k1 [4 sts]

Keep working on 4 sts I-cord for 5cm (2in) to make a stem.

Cut yarn. Using a tapestry needle, thread through the remaining stitches. Pull tightly.

Tie a knot with the stem, the same as for the grapefruit pouch (page 8).

With a long tail from the beginning, stitch onto the crown a few times, using tapestry needle. Shape it textured.

BROCCOLI BODY

Stretchy Hem (instructions on page 3)

3.25 mm (US3) dpns, light green; work in flat

Provisional CO 37 sts

Change to 4.0 mm (US6) needles; work in flat

R1 (WS): p2, (k1, p1)*, rep* to last 1 st, p1

R2 (RS): k2, (p1, k1)*, rep* to the last 1 st, pm, join in round. Move the last 1 st to the left needle.

Work in round from now onward.

R3: k2tog (the last 1 st from R2 and the first st from R3), k to BOR [36 sts]

R4–R9: work in pattern in round (knit the knits, purl the purls).

R10: k in round

Connect dark green.

R11: [(with light green) k2, (with dark green) k2]*, rep* to BOR

R12: [(with light green) k2, (with dark green) kfb x 2]*, rep* to BOR [54 sts]

R13: [(with light green) k2, (with dark green) k4]*, rep* to BOR

Cut light green yarn. Work with dark green yarn only from now onward.

R14: k4, M1, (k6, M1) x 8, k2 [63 sts]

R15: p in round

R16: k5, M1, (k7, M1) x 8, k2 [72 sts]

K17: p in round

R18: k in round

R19: p in round

R20: (k4, k2tog)*, rep* to BOR [60 sts]

R21–R23: rep. R17–R19

R24: (k3, k2tog)*, rep* to BOR [48 sts]

R25–R27: rep R17–R19

R28: (k2, k2tog)*, rep* to BOR [36 sts]

R29: p in round

R30: (k1, k2tog)*, rep* to BOR [24 sts]

R31: p in round

R32: (k2tog)*, rep* to BOR [12 sts]

R33: p in round

R34: (k2tog)*, rep* to BOR [6 sts]

R35: p in round

Cut yarn. Using a tapestry needle, thread through the remaining stitches twice. Pull tightly.

PUMPKIN POUCH

YARN TO USE

The Loop with a Leaf (green)

- sport weight, Shalimar Enzo Sport, loden, 38m

Pumpkin Body (spice)

- worsted weight, Lion Brand Heartland, Yosemite, 52m

Pumpkin Body (beige)

- worsted weight, Bernat Wool-up, caramel tweed, 52m

THE LOOP WITH A LEAF

3.25 mm (US3) dpns, dark green; work in round

CO 3 sts

R1: k3, working as I-cord

R2: (kfb) x 3 [6 sts]

R3: k in round

R4: (k1, M1R, k1, M1L, k1) x 2 [10 sts]

R5: k in round

R6: (k2, M1R, k1, M1L, k2) x 2 [14 sts]

R7: k in round

R8: (k3, M1R, k1, M1L, k3) x 2 [18 sts]

R9: k in round

R10: (k4, M1R, k1, M1L, k4) x 2 [22 sts]

R11: k in round

R12: (k5, M1R, k1, M1L, k5) x 2 [26 sts]

R13: k in round

R14: (k6, M1R, k1, M1L, k6) x 2 [30 sts]

R15: k in round

R16: [(k1, M1R) x 3, k4, M1R, k1, M1L, k4, (M1L, k1) x 3] x 2 [46 sts]

R17: k in round

R18: [(k1, M1R) x 3, k8, M1R, k1, M1L, k8, (M1L, k1) x 3] x 2 [62 sts]

R19: (ssk, k27, k2tog) x 2 [58 sts]

R20: (ssk, k25, k2tog) x 2 [54 sts]

R21: k in round

R22: (ssk, k23, k2tog) x 2 [50 sts]

R23: (ssk, k21, k2tog) x 2 [46 sts]

R24: (ssk, k19, k2tog) x 2 [42 sts]

R25: (ssk, k17, k2tog) x 2 [38 sts]

R26: (ssk, k15, k2tog) x 2 [34 sts]

R27: (ssk, k13, k2tog) x 2 [30 sts]

R28: (ssk, k11, k2tog) x 2 [26 sts]

R29: [(k1, M1R) x 2, k9, (M1L, k1) x 2] x 2 [34 sts]

R30: k in round

R31: (k1, M1R, k15, M1L, k1) x 2 [38 sts]

Work on #1 side and #4 side; work in round, as shown in photos on the next page.

R1: k8 (on #1), place center 3 sts onto pm or yarn scrap, k8 (on #4) in round

R2: ssk, k12, k2tog [14 sts]

R3: ssk, k10, k2tog [12 sts]

R4: ssk x 2, k4, k2tog x 2 [8 sts]

Cut yarn. Using a tapestry needle, thread through the remaining stitches. Pull tightly.

Work on #2 side and #3 side; work in round, as shown in photos.

R1: k8 (on #2), k8 (on #3) in round

R2: k6, k2tog, ssk, k6 [14 sts]

R3: k5, k2tog, ssk, k5 [12 sts]

R4: k2, k2tog x 2, ssk x 2, k2 [8 sts]

Cut yarn. Using a tapestry needle, thread through the remaining stitches. Pull tightly.

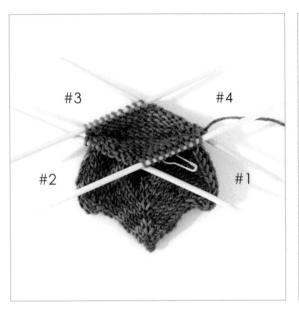 

Place 3 sts from pm or yarn scrap onto 3.25 mm (US3) dpn. Work on 3 sts I-cord for about 40cm (16in).

Join the I-cord with 3 sts from pm on the other side, as shown photo 3 and 4, 6 sts on 1 dpn.

Keep working on I-cord.

Next R: (k2tog) x 3 [3 sts]

Next 5 rows, 3 sts I-cord

Next R: k1, kfb, k1 [4 sts]

Keep working on 4 sts I-cord for 5cm (2in) to make a stem.

Cut yarn. Using a tapestry needle, thread through the remaining stitches. Pull tightly.

Tie a knot with the stem, the same as for grapefruit pouch (page 8).

PUMPKIN BODY

Stretchy Hem (instructions on page 3)

3.25 mm (US3) dpns, dark green; work in flat

Provisional CO 35 sts

Change to 4.0 mm (US6) needles, pumpkin color; work in flat

R1 (WS): p to EOR [35 sts]

R2 (RS): sl1p, k2, pm, (p1, k1tbl, p1, k4, pm) x 4, (p1, k1tbl) x 2 [35 sts]

R3 (WS): sl1p, k1, p1tbl, k1, (p4, k1, p1tbl, k1) x 4, p2, p1tbl

R4 (RS): sl1p, (M1L, k1) x 2, (p1, k1tbl, p1, k1, M1R, k2, M1L, k1) x 4, p1, k1tbl, p1, M1R, k1tbl [46 sts]

R5 (WS): sl1p, p1, k1, p1tbl, k1, (p6, k1, p1tbl, k1) x 4, p4, p1tbl

R6 (RS): sl1p, k1, (k1, M1L) x 2, k1, [p1, k1tbl, p1, (k1, M1R) x 2, k2, (M1L, k1) x 2] x 4, p1, k1tbl, p1, M1R, k1, M1R, k1tbl [66 sts]

R7 (WS): sl1p, p3, k1, p1tbl, k1, (p10, k1, p1tbl, k1) x 4, p6, p1tbl

R8 (RS): sl1p, (k2, M1L) x 2, k2, [p1, k1tbl, p1, (k2, M1R) x 2, (k2, M1L) x 2, k2] x 4, p1, k1tbl, p1, k2, M1R, k1, M1R, k1tbl [86 sts]

R9 (WS): sl1p, p5, k1, p1tbl, k1, (p14, k1, p1tbl, k1) x 4, p8, p1tbl

R10 (RS): sl1p, k8, (p1, k1tbl, p1, k14) x 4, p1, k1tbl, p1, k5, k1tbl [86 sts]

R11–R14: rep R9–R10

R15 (WS): rep R9

R16 (RS): work in pattern to the last 1 st; join as a round. Move the last 1 st to the left needle; k2tog, k8, pm

Work in round from now onward.

R17–R27: work in pattern [85 sts]

R28: (p1, k1tbl, p1, k1, ssk, k8, k2tog, k1) x 5 [75 sts]

R29: work in pattern

R30: (p1, k1tbl, p1, k1, ssk, ssk, k2, k2tog, k2tog, k1) x 5 [55 sts]

R31: work in pattern

R32: (CDD, k2, ssk, k2tog, k2) x 5 [35 sts]

R33: work in pattern

R34: (k1, ssk, k2, k2tog) x 5 [25 sts]

R35: work in pattern

R36: (ssk, k1, k2tog) x 5 [15 sts]

R37: work in pattern

Cut yarn. Using a tapestry needle, thread through the remaining stitches. Pull tightly.

ACORN POUCHES

YARN TO USE

White Oak Acorn (long narrower shape, dark brown, on left in the photo)

- worsted weight, Bernat Wool-up Worsted, taupe heather,35.5m for the acorn cap
- worsted weight, Bernat Wool-up Worsted, brown, 23m for the acorn fruit

Red Oak Acorn (shorter round shape, rust brown, on right in the photo)

- worsted weight, Patons Wool Classic Worsted, heath heather, 37m for the acorn cap
- worsted weight, Knitting for Olive Heavy Merino, rust, 27m for acorn fruit

String with an oak leaf, any of acorn cap colors, 15m

THE STRING WITH AN OAK LEAF

3.25 mm (US3) dpns, beige or light brown; work in flat

CO 3 sts, work on I-cord for 45cm (18in).

R1 (WS): same as working on I-cord, pull yarn, CO 9 sts using a cable method [12 sts]

R2 (RS): k12, CO 9 sts using a cable method (see "Techniques" on page 114) [21 sts]

R3 (WS): k9, p1, sl1p, p1, k9

R4 (RS): k1, kfb, k7, CDD, k9 [20 sts]

R5 (WS): k1, kfb, k7, sl1p wyif, k10 [21 sts]

R6 (RS): k9, CDD, k9 [19 sts]

R7 (WS): k9, sl1p wyif, k9

R8 (RS): BO 1 st, k6, CDD, k8 [16 sts]

R9 (WS): BO 1 st, k6, sl1p wyif, k7, CO 4 sts [19 sts]

R10 (RS): k10, CDD, k6, CO 4 sts [21 sts]

R11 (WS): k10, sl1p wyif, k10

R12 (RS): k1, kfb, k7, CDD, k9 [20 sts]

R13 (WS): k1, kfb, k7, sl1p wyif, k10 [21 sts]

R14 (RS): k9, CDD, k9 [19 sts]

R15 (WS): k9, sl1p wyif, k9

R16 (RS): BO 1 st, k6, CDD, k8 [16 sts]

R17 (WS): BO 1 st, k6, sl1p wyif, k7, CO 4 sts [19 sts]

R18 (RS): k10, CDD, k6, CO 4 sts [21 sts]

R19 (WS): k10, sl1p wyif, k10

R20 (RS): k9, CDD, k9 [19 sts]

R21 (WS): k9, sl1p wyif, k9

R22 (RS): k8, CDD, k8 [17 sts]

R23 (WS): k8, sl1p wyif, k8

R24 (RS): BO 1 st, k5, CDD, k7 [14 sts]

R25 (WS): BO 1 st, k5, sl1p wyif, k6 [13 sts]

R26 (RS): k5, CDD, k5 [11 sts]

R27 (WS): k5, sl1p wyif, k5

R28 (RS): k4, CDD, k4 [9 sts]

R29 (WS): k4, sl1p wyif, k4

R30 (RS): k3, CDD, k3 [7 sts]

R31 (WS): k3, sl1p wyif, k3

R32 (RS): k2, CDD, k2 [5 sts]

R33 (WS): k2, sl1p wyif, k2

R34(RS): k1, CDD, k1 [3 sts]

R35 (WS): k1, sl1p wyif, k1

R36 (RS): CDD [1 st]

Cut yarn. Using a tapestry needle, thread through the remaining stitches. Pull tightly.

WHITE OAK ACORN

Stretchy Hem (instructions on page 3)

3.25 mm (US3) dpns, beige or light brown; work in flat

Provisional CO 37 sts

ACORN CAP

Change to 4.0 mm (US6) needles; work in flat.

R1 (WS): p to EOR [37 sts]

R2 (RS): k1, (M1, k3)*, rep* to EOR [49 sts]

R3 (WS): (p1, k1)*, rep* to the last 1 st, p1

R4 (RS): k to EOR

R5 (WS): rep. R3

R6 (RS): k2, (M1, k4)*, rep* to the last 3 sts, M1, k3 [61 sts]

R7 (WS): [(p1, k1) x 2, (p2, k1) x 2]*, rep* to the last 1 st, p1

R8 (RS): k to EOR

R9 (WS): rep. R7

R10 (RS): k3, (M1, k10)*, rep* to the last 8 sts, M1, k8 [67 sts]

R11 (WS): [(p1, k1) x 2, p2, k1, p3, k1]*, rep* to the last 1 st, p1

R12 (RS): k to EOR

R13 (WS): p to EOR

R14 (RS): k to the last 1 st, place pm. Join in round. Move the last 1 st to the left needle.

Work in round.

R15: k2tog, k to BOR [66 sts]

BO

ACORN FRUIT

4.0 mm (US6) needles, contrasting color; work in round

Place the cap upside down, from inside. Pick up 66 sts along the R14 above.

R1–R5: k in round

R6: (k9, k2tog)*, rep* to BOR [60 sts]

R7–R10: k in round

R11: (k8, k2tog)*, rep* to BOR [54 sts]

R12–R14: k in round

R15: (k7, k2tog)*, rep* to BOR [48 sts]

R16–R17: k in round

R18: (k6, k2tog)*, rep* to BOR [42 sts]

R19: k in round

R20: (k5, k2tog)*, rep* to BOR [36 sts]

R21: (k4, k2tog)*, rep* to BOR [30 sts]

R22: (k3, k2tog)*, rep* to BOR [24 sts]

R23: (k2tog)*, rep* to BOR [12 sts]

R24–R25: k in round

Cut yarn. Using a tapestry needle, thread through the remaining stitches. Pull tightly.

RED OAK ACORN

Stretchy Hem (instructions on page 3)

3.25 mm (US3) dpns, light brown; work in flat

Provisional CO 37 sts

ACORN CAP

Change to 4.0 mm (US6) needles; work in flat.

R1 (WS): p to EOR [37 sts]

R2 (RS): k1, (M1, k3)*, rep* to EOR [49 sts]

R3 (WS): (p1, k1)*, rep* to the last 1 st, p1

R4 (RS): k to EOR

R5 (WS): rep R3

R6 (RS): k2, (M1, k4)*, rep* to last 3 sts, M1, k3 [61 sts]

R7 (WS): [(p1, k1) x 2, (p2, k1) x 2]*, rep* to the last 1 st, p1

R8 (RS): k to EOR

R9 (WS): rep R7

R10 (RS): k3, (M1, k5)*, rep* to the last 3 sts, M1, k3 [73 sts]

R11 (WS): (p1, k1) x 2, (k1, p2, k1, p3, k1, p1, k1, p1, k1) x 5, (k1, p2) x 2, p1, k1, p1

R12 (RS): k to EOR

R13 (WS): rep R11

R14–R17: rep R12–R13

R18 (RS): k to the last 1 st, place pm, join in round. Move the last 1 st to the left needle.

Work in round.

R19: k2tog, k to BOR

R20: k in round

BO

ACORN FRUIT

4.0 mm (US6) needles, contrasting color; work in round

Place the cap upside down. From inside, pick up 68 sts (pick up 17 sts, skip 1 st) along the R18 above, as shown in photo.

R1–R10: k in round [68 sts]

R11: (k15, k2tog)*, rep* to BOR [64 sts]

R12–R15: k in round

R16: (k2, k2tog)*, rep* to BOR [48 sts]

R17–R18: k in round

R19: (k1, k2tog)*, rep* to BOR [32 sts]

R20–R21: k in round

R22: (k2tog)*, rep* to BOR [16 sts]

R23–R24: k in round

R25: (k2tog)*, rep* to BOR [8 sts]

R26–R27: k in round

Cut yarn. Using a tapestry needle thread through the remaining stitches. Pull tightly.

CORN POUCH

YARN TO USE

Corn Husks (light green)

- sport weight, Sugar Bush Bliss, mint, 42 m.

Corn (light yellow)

- sport weight, Loop & Threads Snuggly Wuggly Dip Dye, daffodils, 48 m.

THE STRING WITH A MINI CORN

3.25 mm (US3) dpns, light green; work in round

CO 3 sts, work on I-cord for 40-45cm (16-18in).

R1: (kfb) x 3 [6 sts]

R2: k in round

R3: (k1, M1L, k1, M1R, k1) x 2 [10 sts]

R4: k in round

R5: (k2, M1L, k1, M1R, k2) x 2 [14 sts]

R6: k in round

R7: (k3, M1L, k1, M1R, k3) x 2 [18 sts]

R8–R10: k in round

Connect yellow or any corn color.

R11: [(green) k4, (yellow) k1, (green) k4] x 2

R12: [(green) k3, (yellow) k3, (green) k3] x 2

R13: [(green) k2, (yellow) k5, (green) k2] x 2

R14: [(green) k1, (yellow) k7, (green) k1] x 2

Cut green yarn. Work with yellow yarn only from now onward.

Fill with cotton stuffing or yarn scrap.

R15: k in round

R16: (k3, CDD, k3) x 2 [14 sts]

R17: k in round

R18: (k2, CDD, k2) x 2 [10 sts]

R19: k in round

R20: (k1, CDD, k1) x 2 [6 sts]

R21: k in round

Cut yarn. Using a tapestry needle, thread through the remaining stitches. Pull tightly.

CORN BODY

Stretchy Hem (instructions on page 3)

3.25 mm (US3) dpns, green; work in flat

Provisional CO 25 sts

CORN HUSK

Change to 4.0 mm (US6) needles; work in flat

R1 (WS): p to EOR [25 sts]

R2 (RS): k1, (M1L, k3)*, rep* to EOR [33 sts]

R3 (WS): p to EOR

R4 (RS): k1, (M1L, k4)*, rep* to EOR [41 sts]

R5 (WS): p to EOR

R6 (RS): k1, (M1L, k5)*, rep* to EOR [49 sts]

R7 (WS): p to EOR

R8 (RS): k1, (M1L, k6)*, rep* to EOR [57 sts]

R9 (WS): p to EOR

R10 (RS): k19, pm k18, pm, k20 (always slipping pms)

R11 (WS): p to EOR

R12(RS): k to the last 1 st, place main pm; join in round. Move the last 1 st to the left needle.

Work in round from now onward.

R13: k2tog, k to BOR [56 sts]

R14–R15: k in round

SPLIT CORN HUSK INTO THREE

Work on initial 19 sts first, then middle 18 sts, and the last 19 sts separately.

Work in flat on each husk.

THE FIRST HUSK

R1 (RS): (k1, p1) x 2, k11, (p1, k1) x 2, turn work [19 sts]

R2 (WS): sl1p, k1, p1, k1, p11, (k1, p1) x 2 [19 sts]

R3 (RS): sl1p, p1, k1, p1, ssk, k to the last 6 sts, k2tog, (p1, k1) x 2 [17 sts]

R4 (WS): sl1p, k1, p1, k1, p to the last 4sts, (k1, p1) x 2

R5–R10: rep R3–R4 [11 sts]

R11 (RS): sl1p, p1, k1, p1, CDD, (p1, k1) x 2 [9 sts]

R12 (WS): sl1p, (k1, p1) x 4

R13 (RS): sl1p, p1, k1, CDD, k1, p1, k1 [7 sts]

R14 (WS): sl1p, k1, p3, k1, p1

R15 (RS): sl1p, p1, CDD, p1, k1 [5 sts]

R16 (WS): sl1p, (k1, p1) x 2

R17 (RS): sl1p, CDD, k1 [3 sts]

R18 (WS): sl1p, p2

R19(RS): CDD [1 st]

Cut yarn. Using a tapestry needle, thread through the remaining stitches. Pull tightly.

THE MIDDLE HUSK

Work on the middle 18 sts; connect yarn; work in flat.

R1 (RS): k1, p1, kfb, k11, (p1, k1) x 2, turn work [19 sts]

R2–R19, work same as the first husk

THE LAST HUSK

Work on the last 19 sts. Connect yarn; work same as the first husk.

CORN

4.0 mm (US6) dpns, yellow or any corn color; work in round

Place inside out, upside down. From where corn husk is joined, pick up 57 sts from inside. Pick up and work direction from right to left.

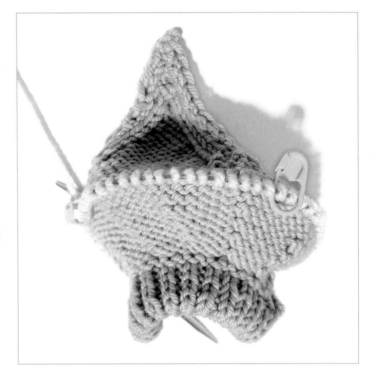

R1: (p17, p2tog) x 3 [54 sts]

R2: p in round

R3: (k1, p2)*, rep* to BOR

R4: (k1, YO, k2, pass YO st over 2 knitted sts after YO)*, rep* to BOR

R5–R22: rep R3–R4

Switch needle to 3.25 mm (US3)

R23–R26: rep R3–R4

R27: (k1, p2tog)*, rep* to BOR [36 sts]

R28: (k1, YO, k1, pass YO st over 1 knitted st after YO)*, rep* to BOR

R29: (k1, p1)*, rep* to BOR

R30: (k1, YO, k1, pass YO st over 1 knitted st after YO)*, rep* to BOR

R31–R34: rep R29–R30

R35: (p2tog)*, rep* to BOR [18 sts]

R36: p in round

Cut yarn. Using a tapestry needle, thread through the remaining stitches twice. Pull tightly.

CHESTNUT POUCH

YARN TO USE

Spiny Burr

- sport weight, Lanecardate Camel, greggio, 73m

Chestnut

- sport or light DK weight (hold 2 stands of fingering-weight yarn together), 55m

1. fingering weight, All for Yarn, hand-dyed, red cedar bark
2. fingering weight, Jamieson & Smith Shetland 2-ply, FC38

THE STRING WITH A CHESTNUT

3.25 mm (US3) dpns, brown or any chestnut color; work in round

CO 3 sts, work on I-cord for 35-40cm (16-18in).

R1: (kfb) x 3 [6 sts]

R2: k in round

R3: (k1, M1R, k1, M1L, k1) x 2 [10 sts]

R4: k in round

R5: (k1, M1R, k3, M1L, k1) x 2 [14 sts]

R6: k in round

R7: (k1, M1R, k5, M1L, k1) x 2 [18 sts]

R8: k in round

R9: (k1, M1R, k7, M1L, k1) x 2 [22 sts]

R10: k in round

R11: (k1, M1R, k9, M1L, k1) x 2 [26 sts]

R12–R14: k in round

R15: (k1, ssk, k7, k2tog, k1) x 2 [22 sts]

Change yarn color.

R16: k in round

R17: p1, k2tog, [(p1, k1) x 2], (p1, k2tog) x 2, [(p1, k1) x 3], p1, k2tog [18 sts]

R18: (k1, p1)*, rep* to BOR

R19: k2tog, [(p1, k1) x 2], p1, k2tog, p2tog, [(k1, p1) x 2], k1, p2tog [14 sts]

R20: (p1, k1)*, rep* to BOR

Cut yarn. Using a tapestry needle, thread through the remaining stitches. Pull tightly.

CHESTNUT BODY

Stretchy Hem (instructions on page 3)

3.25 mm (US3) dpns, light brown; work in flat

Provisional CO 31 sts

SPINY BURR

Change to 4.0 mm (US6) needles; work in flat.

R1 (WS): p to EOR [25 sts]

R2 (RS): (k3, M1L) x 10, k1 [41 sts]

R3 (WS): sl1p, p to EOR

R4 (RS): sl1p, k3, M1L, (k4, M1L) x 9, k1 [51 sts]

R5 (WS): sl1p, k to EOR

R6 (RS): sl1p, (k1, loop1) x 2, M1L, [(loop1, k1) x 2, Loop1, M1L] x 9, k1 [61 sts]

(see "Techniques" on page 116)

R7 (WS): sl1p, k to EOR

R8 (RS): sl1p, k2, loop1, k1, loop1, M1L, [(k1, loop1) x 6, M1L] x 4, (k1, loop1) x 2, k2, M1L, k1 [67 sts]

R9 (WS): sl1p, k to EOR

R10 (RS): sl1p, (k1, loop1)*, rep* to the last 2 sts, k2

R11 (WS): sl1p, k to EOR

R12 (RS): sl1p, k1, (k1, loop1)*, rep* to the last 3 sts, k2, pm; join in round. Move the last 1st to the left needle.

Work in round from now onward.

R13: p2tog, p to BOR [66 sts]

R14: (loop1, k1)*, rep* to BOR

R15: p to BOR

R16: (k1, loop1)*, rep* to BOR

R17: p to BOR

SPLIT SPINY BURR INTO THREE

Work on initial 22 sts first, then middle 22 sts, and the last 22 sts separately.

Work in flat.

The First Part

R1 (RS): k2, (loop1, k1)*, rep* to the last 2 sts, k2, turn work [22 sts]

R2 (WS): sl1p, k21

R3 (RS): sl1p, k2, (loop1, k1)*, rep* to the last 1 st, k1

R4 (WS): sl1p, k to EOR

R5 (RS): sl1p, k1, (loop1, k1)*, rep* to the last 2 sts, k2

R6 (WS): sl1p, k2tog, k to the last 3 sts, ssk, k1 [20 sts]

R7–R16: rep. R5–R6 [10 sts]

R17 (RS): sl1p, k1, (loop1, k1)*, rep* to the last 2 sts, k2

R18 (WS): sl1p, (k2tog, k1) x 2, ssk, k1 [7 sts]

R19 (RS): sl1p, (k1, loop1) x 2, k2

R20 (WS): sl1p, k2tog, k1, ssk, k1 [5 sts]

R21 (RS): sl1p, k to EOR

Cut yarn. Using a tapestry needle, thread through the remaining stitches. Pull tightly.

For the middle and the last parts, connect yarn; work the same as the first part.

CHESTNUT

4.0 mm (US6) dpns, brown or any chestnut color; work in round

Place inside out. From where chestnut spiny burr is joined, pick up 66 sts from inside.

R1–R19: k in round

R20: (k4, k2tog) x 11 [55 sts]

R21–R22: k in round

R23: (k3, k2tog) x 11 [44 sts]

R24–R25: k in round

R26: (k2, k2tog) x 11 [33 sts]

R27–R28: k in round

R29: (k1, k2tog) x 11 [22 sts]

R30: k in round

R31: (k2tog) x 11 [11 sts]

R32: (k2tog) x 3, k1, (k2tog) x 2 [6 sts]

R33: k in round

Cut yarn. Using a tapestry needle, thread through the remaining stitches. Pull tightly.

· ·

PART II

VEGETABLE PATTERNS

You could read the best kind of book and sip a warm cup of coffee—or you could chuckle a little while knitting a head of garlic.

Dear friend,

Watching my garden grow, steadily and quietly, brought me newfound joy. Naturally, I picked up my yarn and started knitting these delightful little projects. I tried as closely as I could to capture their true forms and colors, each unique in its own beauty.

As I knitted, I burst into laughter, picturing myself sitting alone, making these funny creations. May they bring whimsy and sustenance to your life, as they have for me.

Wishing you peace,

YUN

This part, knitting 3-D toy vegetables, starts with a small number of stitches. You will knit in the round, using double-point needles, seamlessly. You can change the color and vary the yarn to make your own interpretations of vegetables.

These are the materials needed to make the knitted vegetable in this book.

WHAT TO USE FOR MAKING VEGETABLES

Knitting Needles

4.0 mm (US6) set of double-point needles

3.25 mm (US3) set of double-point needles

2.5 mm (US1.5) set of double-point needles (optional for tighter-looking stitches)

Yarn

fingering, sport, DK, worsted weight yarn scraps

You can substitute any yarn you have on hand; just make sure they are the same weight.

You can hold two strands of different yarn together for variegated-color works.

Notions

- place marker, to place at the beginning of the round when you work in round
- tapestry needle for finishing, weaving the tails in
- cotton stuffing or yarn scraps

POTATOES

It is fascinating how root vegetables can grow in abundance under the ground. What could grow in the dark? My heart skips a beat as I harvest the unfolding mysteries of odd shapes, delightful colors, and sizes of yams and potatoes.

YARN TO USE

- sport or DK weight, yarn scraps, small (large) potatoes, 16 (21)m

SMALL POTATO

3.25 mm (US3) dpns, beige, yellow, or red—any of your favorite potato colors; work in round

CO 4 sts

R1: (kfb) x 4 [8 sts]

R2: (kfb, k1) x 4 [12 sts]

R3: (k2, kfb) x 4 [16 sts]

R4: k in round

R5: (kfb, k3) x 4 [20 sts]

R6: k in round

R7: (k3, kfb) x 5 [25 sts]

R8: k in round

R9: (kfb, k4) x 5 [30 sts]

R10–R16: k in round

R17: (k4, k2tog) x 5 [25 sts]

R18: (k2tog, k3) x 5 [20 sts]

R19: k in round

R20: (k3, k2tog) x 4 [16 sts]

R21: k to the last 2 sts, k2tog [15 sts]

R22: (k3, k2tog) x 3 [12 sts]

Fill with cotton stuffing or yarn scraps.

Cut yarn about 20-25cm (8-10in) long. Using a tapestry needle, thread through the remaining stitches. Pull tightly. With a long tail, stitch on to potato a few times to make eyes.

BIG POTATO

CO 4 sts

R1–R11: work same as the small potato [30 sts]

R12: (k5, kfb) x 5 [35 sts]

R13–R14: k in round

R15: k4, (kfb, k6) x 4, k3 [39 sts]

R16–R20: k in round

R21: (k4, k2tog) x 6, k3 [33 sts]

R22: k in round

R23: (k2tog, k3) x 6, k2tog, k1 [26 sts]

R24: k in round

R25: (k2, k2tog) x 6, k2 [20 sts]

R26: k to the last 2 sts, k2tog [19 sts]

R27: (k3, k2tog) x 3, k4 [16 sts]

Fill with cotton stuffing or yarn scraps.

R28: (k2tog) x 8 [8 sts]

Cut yarn about 20-25cm (8-10in) long. Using a tapestry needle, thread through the remaining stitches. Pull tightly. With a long tail, stitch onto potato a few times to make eyes.

YAMS

YARN TO USE

- sport or DK weight, yarn scrap, small (large) yams, 16 (24)m

SMALL YAM

3.25 mm (US3) dpns; red, purple, or any yam color; work in round

CO 6 sts

R1: k in round

R2: (kfb, k2) x 2 [8 sts]

R3: k2, kfb, k to BOR [9 sts]

R4: k7, kfb, k1 [10 sts]

R5: (k3, kfb) x 2, k2 [12 sts]

R6: (k2, kfb) x 4 [16 sts]

R7: (k3, kfb) x 4 [20 sts]

R8–R11: k in round

R12: k3, kfb, k to BOR [21 sts]

R13: k4, k2tog, k6, kfb, k7, kfb [22 sts]

R14: (k6, kfb) x 2, k7, kfb [25 sts]

R15: k5, kfb, k4, kfb, (k5, kfb) x 2, kfb, k1 [30 sts]

R16: (k10, kfb) x 2, k8 [32 sts]

R17–R18: k in round

R19: k2tog, k to BOR [31 sts]

R20–R21: k in round

R22: k to the last 2 sts, k2tog [30 sts]

R23: k in round

R24: k to the last 2 sts, k2tog [29 sts]

R25: (k4, k2tog, k5, k2tog) x 2, k3 [25 sts]

R26: k to the last 2 sts, k2tog [24 sts]

R27: k in round

R28: (k2tog, k5) x 3, k3 [21 sts]

Fill with cotton stuffing or yarn scraps.

R29: k in round

R30: (k2, k2tog) x 5, k1 [16 sts]

R31: (k2, k2tog) x 4 [12 sts]

R32: k5, k2tog, k5 [11 sts]

R33: (k1, k2tog) x 3, k2 [8 sts]

R34–R35: k to the last 2 sts, k2tog [6 sts]

Cut yarn about 20-25cm (8-10in) long. Using a tapestry needle, thread through the remaining stitches. Pull tightly. With a long tail, stitch on to yam a few times to make dimples.

BIG YAM

CO 6 sts

R1–R13: work the same as the small yam [22 sts]

R14: k in round

R15: (k6, kfb) x 2, k7, kfb [25 sts]

R16: k in round

R17: k5, kfb, k4, kfb, (k5, kfb) x 2, k2 [29 sts]

R18: (k10, kfb) x 2, k7 [31 sts]

R19–R20: k in round

R21: k2tog, k to the last 1 st, kfb

R22: k14, kfb, k to BOR [32 sts]

R23: k2tog, k to BOR [31 sts]

R24: k3, kfb, k to BOR [32 sts]

R25: k in round

R26: k7, kfb, k to BOR [33 sts]

R27: k to the last 2 sts, k2tog [32 sts]

R28: k in round

R29: k to the last 2 sts, k2tog [31 sts]

R30: (k5, k2tog) x 4, k3 [27 sts]

R31: k in round

R32: k to the last 2 sts, k2tog [26 sts]

R33: k in round

R34: (k2tog, k6) x 3, k2tog [22 sts]

R35: k in round

R36: (k2, k2tog) x 5, k2 [17 sts]

R37: k in round

R38: (k3, k2tog) x 3, k2tog [13 sts]

R39: k5, k2tog, k6 [12 sts]

Fill with cotton stuffing or yarn scraps.

R40: (k1, k2tog) x 4 [8 sts]

R41: k in round

R42–R43: k to the last 2 sts, k2tog [6 sts]

R44: k in round

Cut yarn about -25cm (8-10in) long. Using a tapestry needle, thread through the remaining stitches. Pull tightly. With a long tail, stitch onto yam a few times to make dimples.

EGGPLANT

If you are a big fan of eggplant, both knitted and fresh, I'd like to introduce "12 Easy Eggplant Recipes" from *The Love & Lemons Cookbook*: www.loveandlemons.com/easy-eggplant-recipes.

YARN TO USE

- DK or worsted weight, purple yarn scrap, long (chubby) eggplants, 28 (30)m
- DK weight, green yarn scrap, 2m

LONG EGGPLANT

4.0 mm (US6) dpns, purple; work in round

CO 6 sts

R1: (k2, M1) x 3 [9 sts]

R2: k in round

R3: (k3, M1) x 3 [12 sts]

R4: (k4, M1) x 3 [15 sts]

R5: (k5, M1) x 3 [18 sts]

R6: (k6, M1) x 3 [21 sts]

R7: (k7, M1) x 3 [24 sts]

R8: k in round

R9: (k8, M1) x 3 [27 sts]

R10–R17: k in round

R18: k7, k2tog, k to BOR [26 sts]

R19: k in round

R20: k15, k2tog, k9 [25 sts]

R21: k in round

R22: k to the last 2 sts, k2tog [24 sts]

R23: k in round

R24: k6, k2tog, k to BOR [23 sts]

R25: k in round

R26: k13, k2tog, k8 [22 sts]

R27: k in round

R28: k to the last 2 sts, k2tog [21 sts]

R29: k in round

R30: k5, k2tog, k to BOR [20 sts]

R31: k in round

R32: k11, k2tog, k7 [19 sts]

R33: k in round

R34: k to the last 2 sts, k2tog [18 sts]

R35–R40: k in round

Fill with cotton stuffing or yarn scraps.

Connect green.

R41: [(green) k1, (purple) k2] x 6

R42: [(green) k2, (purple) k1] x 6

Cut purple; work with green only.

R43: k in round

R44: (k1, k2tog) x 6 [12 sts]

R45: k in round

Change needle to 3.25 mm (US3) dpns

R46: (k2tog) x 6 [6 sts]

R47: k in round

R48: (k2tog) x 3 [3 sts]

R49: k in round

R50: k1, k2tog [2 sts]

R51: k2

Cut yarn. Using a tapestry needle, thread through the remaining stitches. Pull tightly.

CHUBBY EGGPLANT

4.0 mm (US6) dpns, purple; work in round

CO 6 sts

R1: k in round

R2: (k1, M1) x 6 [12 sts]

R3: k in round

R4: (k1, M1) x 12 [24 sts]

R5: k in round

R6: (k4, M1) x 6 [30 sts]

R7: k in round

R8: (k5, M1) x 6 [36 sts]

R9–R15: k in round

R16: (k10, k2tog) x 3 [33 sts]

R17: k in round

R18: (k9, k2tog) x 3 [30 sts]

R19: k in round

R20: (k8, k2tog) x 3 [27 sts]

R21–R22: k in round

R23: (k7, k2tog) x 3 [24 sts]

R24–R25: k in round

R26: (k6, k2tog) x 2, k8 [22 sts]

R27: k in round

R28: (k5, k2tog) x 2, k8 [20 sts]

R29: k in round

R30: (k4, k2tog) x 2, k8 [18 sts]

R31–R36: k in round

R37: (k3, k2tog) x 2, k8 [16 sts]

Change needles to 3.25 mm (US3) dpns.

R38: k in round

Fill with cotton stuffing or yarn scraps.

Connect green.

R39: [(green) k1, (purple) k3] x 4

R40: [(green) k2, (purple) k2] x 4

Cut purple; work with green only.

R41: (k2, k2tog) x 4 [12 sts]

R42: k in round

R43: (k2tog) x 6 [6 sts]

R44: k in round

R45: (k2tog) x 3 [3 sts]

R46: k in round

R47: k1, k2tog [2 sts]

R48: k2

Cut yarn. Using a tapestry needle, thread through the remaining stitches. Pull tightly.

CUCUMBER

As I knitted the bell peppers and cucumber, my mouth watered. Pickles! So crunchy, so sour or sweet. I craved a bite.

Here's my recipe for sweet cucumber pickles:

Ingredients

    3 cucumbers,
    1/4 red cabbage,
    1 onion,
    3 bell peppers
    1/2 lemon

Ingredients for pickling brine

    4 cups of water
    2 cups of vinegar
    1 1/2 cups of white sugar
    1 tablespoon of salt
    1 tablespoon of pickle spice (optional)
    2–3 bay leaves

Wash and cut vegetables into bite-size pieces.

Slice the lemon.

Prepare 2 clean jars (1 liter each).

Heat the pickling brine until it boils.

Put vegetables and sliced lemon in jars. Pour in hot pickling brine. Wait until it cools down.

Place in the fridge for 2–3 days before eating.

Bon appétit!

YARN TO USE

- sport or DK weight, Shalimar Enzo Sport, loden, 21m

CUCUMBER

3.25 mm (US3) dpns, green; work in round

CO 6 sts

R1: (k1, kfb) x 3 [9 sts]

R2: (k2, kfb) x 3 [12 sts]

R3: k in round

R4: (k1, kfb) x 6 [18 sts]

R5: k in round

R6: (k2, kfb) x 6 [24 sts]

R7: k in round

R8: k2tog, k to BOR [23 sts]

R9: k in round

R10: k5, k2tog, k to BOR [22 sts]

R11: k in round

R12: k10, k2tog, k to BOR [21 sts]

R13: k15, k2tog, k to BOR [20 sts]

R14: (k3, p1) x 5

R15: k in round

R16: k1, (p1, k3) x 4, p1, k2

R17: k in round

R18–R37: rep. R14–R17

R38: (k4, kfb) x 4 [24 sts]

R39–R42: k in round

R43: (k2, k2tog) x 6 [18 sts]

R44: k in round

Fill with cotton stuffing or yarn scraps.

R45: (k2tog) x 9 [9 sts]

R46: k in round

Cut yarn. Using a tapestry needle, thread through the remaining stitches. Pull tightly.

BELL PEPPERS

YARN TO USE

- sport or DK weight, yarn scrap, small (large) bell peppers, 20 (26)m
- sport or DK weight, yarn scrap, green, 2-3m

SMALL BELL PEPPER

4.0 mm (US6) dpns, green; work in round

Stem

CO 7 sts

R1–R2: k in round

R3: k to the last 2 sts, k2tog [6 sts]

R4–R6: k in round

R7: kfb x 6 [12 sts]

R8: (k3, kfb, k2) x 2 [14 sts]

Change to yellow or any bell pepper color.

R9: (k1, kfb) x 7 [21 sts]

R10: (kfb, k2) x 7 [28 sts]

R11: k in round

Rearrange sts: 10/10/8 sts on each dpn

R12: k1B, k3, kfb, kfb, k4 / k1B, k3, kfb, k5 / k1B, k2, kfb, kfb, k3 [12/11/10 sts on each dpn]

R13: k in round

R14: k1B, k2, kfb, k3 kfb, k4 / k1B, k2, kfb, k3, kfb, k3 / k1B, k4, kfb, k4 [14/13/11 sts]

R15: (k5, kfb) x 2 times, k2 / k5, kfb, kfb, k6 / k4, kfb, k1, kfb, k4 [16/15/13 sts]

R16: (k1B, kfb, k to the last 1 st of the needle, kfb) x 3 [18/17/15 sts]

R17: (k to the last 2 sts, k2tog) x 3 [17/16/14 sts]

R18: (k1B, k to the end of the needle) x 3

R19: k2, k2tog, k5, k2tog, k6 / k2, k2tog, k8, k2tog, k2 / k2, k2tog, k6, k2tog, k2 [15/14/12 sts]

R20: (k1B, k to the end of the needle) x 3

R21: k in round

R22: k1B, k1, k2tog, k9, k2tog / k1B, k1, k2tog, k2, k2tog, k6 / k1B, k4, k2tog, k5 [13/12/11 sts]

R23: k6, k2tog, k5 / k5, k2tog, k5 / k4, k2tog, k5 [12/11/10 sts]

R24: (k1B, k to the end of the needle) x 3

R25: (k2, k2tog) x 3 / k4, k2tog, k3, k2tog / k4, k2tog, k4 [9/9/9 sts]

R26: (k1B, k to the end of the needle) x 3

R27: k3, k2tog, k4 / k to the end of the needle / k3, k2tog, k4 [8/9/8 sts]

R28: k1B, k3, kfb, k3 / k1B, k4, kfb, k3 / k1B, kfb, k2, kfb, k3 [9/10/10 sts]

R29: k in round

R30: (k1B, k to the end of the needle) x 3

R31–R32: rep. R29–R30

R33: (k2, kfb, k to the end of the needle) x 3 [10/11/11 sts]

R34: (k1B, k to the end of the needle) x 3

R35: k in round

R36: (k1B, k to the end of the needle) x 3

R37: k in round

Fill with cotton stuffing or yarn scraps.

R38: CDD x 10, k2tog [11 sts]

Cut yarn about 30cm (12in) long. Using a tapestry needle, thread through the remaining stitches. Pull tightly. With a long tail:

1. Stick the needle through the bottom until it comes out the top.
2. Pull the yarn downward along the side (k1B made lines) of the pepper toward the bottom; (3) rep (1)–(2), two more times for the small bell pepper; three more times for the large bell pepper.

This will create the crevice on the sides of the peppers.

LARGE BELL PEPPER

4.0 mm (US6) dpns, green; work in round

Stem

CO 7 sts

R1–R11: work the same as the small bell pepper

Rearrange sts: 7 sts on 4 of each dpn

R12: (k1B, k1, kfb, k1, kfb, k2) x 4 [9 sts on each dpn]

R13: k in round

R14: (k1B, k2, kfb, kfb, k4) x 4 [11 sts on each dpn]

R15: (k6, kfb, k4) x 4 [12 sts on each dpn]

R16: (k1B, kfb, k to the last 1 st of the needle, kfb) x 4 [14 sts on each dpn]

R17: k in round

R18: k1B, k6, kfb, k6 / (k1B, k to the end of the needle) x 2 / k1B, k to the last 2 sts, k2tog [15/14/14/13 sts]

R19: (k2, k2tog, k to the last 4 sts of the needle, k2tog, k2) x 4 [13/12/12/11 sts]

R20: (k1B, k to the end of needle) x 4

R21: k8, k2tog, k3 / k3, k2tog, k7 / k2, k2tog, k3, k2tog, k3 / k4, k2tog, k5 [12/11/10/10 sts]

R22: k1B, k6, k2tog, k3 / (k1B, k to the end of needle) x 3 [11/11/10/10 sts]

R23: k6, k2tog, k3 / k1, k2tog, k8 / k5, k2tog, k3 / k3, k2tog, k5 [10/10/9/9 sts]

R24: (k1B, k to the end of needle) x 4

R25: k5, k2tog, k to the end of row [9/10/9/9 sts]

R26: (k1B, k to the end of needle) x 4

R27: k in round

R28: k1B, k3, k2tog, k3 / k1B, k3, k2tog, k4 / k1B, k2tog, k3, k2tog, k1 / k1B, k3, k2tog, k3 [8/9/7/8 sts]

R29: k in round

R30: k1B, k3, kfb, k3 / k1B, k3, k2tog, k3 / k1B, k2, kfb, k3 / k1B, k2, k2tog, k3 [9/8/8/7 sts]

R31: k in round

R32: (k1B, k to the end of needle) x 4

R33: k in round

R34: (k1B, k2, k2tog, k to the end of needle) x 4 [8/7/7/6 sts]

R35–R36: rep. R31–R32

R37: (k2, k2tog) x 2 / (k2, k2tog, k3) x 2 / k to the end of needle [6/6/6/6 sts]

R38: (k1B, k to the end of needle) x 4

R39–R40: k in round

Fill with cotton stuffing or yarn scraps.

R41: CDD x 8 [8 sts]

Cut yarn about 30cm (12in) long. Using a tapestry needle, thread through the remaining stitches. Pull tightly. Shape your pepper in the same way as the small bell peppers.

GREEN ONION

Good things come in threes: green onion, garlic, and chili pepper.

These are the three vegetables you will find in any Korean household. You might as well call them your family. On my mother's annual kimchi-making day, the pungent smell wasn't exactly welcoming when I came home from school. But that thought didn't last long because of the overwhelming gratitude for kimchi that I felt during the cold winter. Now, when the cold wind starts blowing, I remember those days. I can smell the spices on my mother's hands and her kimchi.

YARN TO USE ((OLOR WORKS ORDER)

- fingering or sport weight, Jamieson & Smith Shetland 2-ply, #1 white, 1.5m
- fingering or sport weight, Jamieson & Smith Shetland 2-ply, #202 stone, 2.4m
- fingering or sport weight, Jamieson & Smith Shetland 2-ply, #FC24mix light green, 1.9m
- fingering or sport weight, Jamieson & Smith Shetland 2-ply, #118 moss, 4.7m

GREEN ONION

3.25 mm (US3) dpns, white; work in round

CO 4 sts

R1: kfb x 4 [8 sts]

R2: (kfb, k1) x 4 [12 sts]

R3–R8: k in round

Change to stone or beige.

R9: (k4, k2tog) x 2 [10 sts]

R10–R15: k in round

Fill with cotton stuffing or yarn scraps.

R16: (k3, k2tog) x 2 [8 sts]

R17–R19: k in round

R20: (kfb, k3) x 2 [10 sts]

Connect light green.

R21: [(light green) k1, (stone) k1] x 5

R22: [(stone) k1, (light green) k1] x 5

R23–R24: rep R21–R22

R25: rep R21

Cut stone color.

R26–R30: k in round

Change to dark green.

R31: k in round

R32: (k4, kfb) x 2 [12 sts]

R33–R34: k in round

You will have 4 sts on 3 of each dpn. Work on initial 4 sts I-cord. Connect yarn; work on middle 4 sts I-cord and then the last 4 sts separately, as below.

First green onion leaf: k in round (I-cord) for 7cm (2.5-3in).

Next R: k2, k2tog [3 sts]

Next R: k1, k2tog [2 sts]

Change needles to 2.5 mm (US1.5) (optional for tighter-looking stitches)

Next 2 rows: k2

Cut yarn. Using a tapestry needle, thread through the remaining stitches. Pull tightly.

The second and third green onion leaves: k in round (I-cord) for 5cm (2in).

Next R: k2, k2tog [3 sts]

Next R: k3

Change needles to 2.5 mm (US1.5) (optional for tighter-looking stitches)

Next R: k1, k2tog [2 sts]

Cut yarn. Using a tapestry needle, thread through the remaining stitches. Pull tightly.

HOW TO MAKE ROOTS

- fingering or sport weight, Jamieson & Smith Shetland 2-ply, #FC43 mix, 30cm

1. Place 30 cm. yarn onto a tapestry needle.
2. Make a loop as is shown in the photo for 4–5 times.
3. Wrap the loops a few times and tie a knot.
4. Weave in the tail.

GARLIC

YARN TO USE

- fingering or sport weight, Jamieson & Smith Shetland 2-ply, #202 stone, 11m

GARLIC

3.25 mm (US3) dpns, stone or beige; work in round

CO 6 sts

R1: kfb x 6 [12 sts]

R2: (k1, kfb) x 6 [18 sts]

R3: (k1B, kfb, k1) x 6 [24 sts]

R4: (k2, kfb, k1) x 6 [30 sts]

R5: (k1B, k2, kfb, k1) x 6 [36 sts]

R6: k in round

R7: (k1B, k5) x 6

R8–R11: rep. R6–R7

R12: (k4, k2tog) x 6 [30 sts]

R13: (k1B, k4) x 6

R14: (k1, ssk, k2) x 6 [24 sts]

R15: (k1B, k3) x 6

R16: (k2, k2tog) x 6 [18 sts]

R17: (k1B, k2) x 6

R18: (k1, ssk) x 6 [12 sts]

R19: (k1B, k1) x 6

Fill with cotton stuffing or yarn scrap. Add a strand of pink or light purple yarn on stuffed pouch to look more realistic.

R20: ssk x 6 [6 sts]

R21–R23: k in round

R24: (k2tog, k1) x 2 [4 sts]

R25–R26: k in round

R27: k1, k2tog, k1 [3 sts]

Cut yarn about 30cm (12in) long. Using a tapestry needle, thread through the remaining stitches. Pull tightly. With a long tail:

1. Stick the needle through the bottom until it comes out the top right before the stem.
2. Pull the yarn downward along the side (k1B-made lines) of the garlic toward the bottom, (3) rep (1)–(2), five more times.

This will create the crevice on the sides.

Make garlic roots the same as for green onion (page 100).

CHILI PEPPERS

YARN TO USE ((COLOR WORKS ORDER)

- fingering or sport weight, Jamieson & Smith Shetland 2-ply, #125 copper, small (large) chili peppers, 3.5 (5.5)m
- fingering or sport weight, Jamieson & Smith Shetland 2-ply, #118 moss, 1m

BIG CHILI PEPPER

3.25 mm. (US 3) dpns, red; work in round

CO 3 sts

R1–R2: k in round as I-cord

R3: k1, kfb, k1 [4 sts]

R4: k in round

R5: (k1, kfb) x 2 [6 sts]

R6: k in round

R7: (k1, kfb) x 3 [9 sts]

R8–R9: k in round

R10: (k2, kfb) x 3 [12 sts]

R11–R17: k in round

R18: k5, k2tog, k5 [11 sts]

R19: k6, kfb, k3, kfb [13 sts]

R20: k in round

R21: k1, k2tog, k to BOR [12 sts]

R22: k in round

Fill with cotton stuffing or yarn scraps (optional).

R23: k2tog x 6 [6 sts]

Change to green.

R24: k in round

R25: k2tog x 3 [3 sts]

R26: k1, k2tog [2 sts]

R27–R28: k2 as I-cord

Cut yarn. Using a tapestry needle, thread through the remaining stitches. Pull tightly.

LITTLE CHILI PEPPER

3.25mm (US3) dpns, red; work in round

CO 3 sts

R1–R9: work the same as big chili pepper

R10–R14: k in round

R15: k2tog, k to BOR [8 sts]

R16: k3, k2tog, k3 [7 sts]

R17: k5, k2tog [6 sts]

Change to green.

R18: (k2tog) x 3 [3 sts]

R19: k1, k2tog [2 sts]

R20–R21: k2 as I-cord

Cut yarn. Using a tapestry needle, thread through the remaining stitches. Pull tightly.

Squeeze it with your hand to shape.

ABBREVIATIONS

This section provides abbreviations for the knitting instructions used in this book.

You also easily can find tutorial videos by searching the internet for "abbreviations in knitting."

One of my favorite knitting-tutorial YouTube channels is VeryPink Knits.

BO: bind off

BOR: beginning of the round

CDD: center double decrease: slip next 2 stitches knit-wise together, knit 1 stitch next, and pass two slipped stitches over

CO: cast on

dpn(s): double-point needle(s)

ds: double stitch: slip next stitch and pull yarn over the needle but count as a stitch

EOR: end of row

k: knit

kfb: increase 1 stitch by knitting into front and back of next stitch k1B: knit into next stitch 1 row below

k1tbl: knit 1 stitch through back of loop

k2tog: knit 2 stitches together

mpm: main place marker

M1L: make 1 stitch left by picking up horizontal loop laying before next stitch, inserting needle from front to back and knitting into back of loop

M1R: make 1 stitch right by picking up horizontal loop laying before next stitch. inserting needle from back to front and knitting into front of loop

1st: 1 stitch

1st: first

p: purl

pfkb: purl in the front of the stitch; knit in the back of the same stitch to make 2 stitches from 1 stitch

pm(s): place marker(s)

p1tbl: purl 1 stitch through back loop

p2tog: purl 2 stitches together

R: row

rep: repeat

RS: right side

sl1p: slip 1 stitch purl-wise

ssk: slip next 2 stitches knit-wise one at a time. Pass them back onto left needle; knit through back loop together

st(s): stitch(es)

work in pattern: knit the knits; purl the purls

WS: wrong side

wyif: with yarn in front

YO: yarn over the needle to make 1 extra stitch

TECHNIQUES

LONG-TAIL CAST ON

Leave a tail long enough to cast on the required number of stitches. (One inch per stitch is plenty.) Then:

1. Make a slipknot onto a needle and tighten it.
2. On your left hand, wrap your thumb with tail end and index finger with working yarn connected in a ball. Hold both ends of yarn with your free fingers.
3. Insert the needle from front to back underneath the strand of yarn in front on your thumb and pull toward index finger.
4. Insert the needle from back to front on the yarn strand on your index finger; pull the loop (working yarn) into front through the strand over your thumb.
5. Repeat steps 1 to 4, as many times as you need.

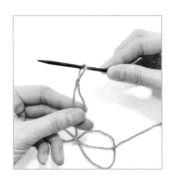   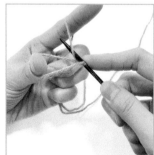

CAST ON USING CABLE METHOD

1. Knit into the first stitch. Bring the new loop to the right, and slip it onto the left needle.

2. Insert the right needle between the two stitches on the left needle.

3. Wrap the yarn around the right needle, and then bring a new loop through the front as knit.

4. Place this loop (stitch) to the left needle.

  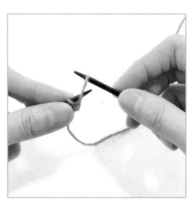

PROVISIONAL CAST ON

It allows you to knit from both sides of each cast-on stitch (top and bottom). Once you've knitted a few rows, the stitches on the scrap of yarn can be put back on needles and knitted in the other direction.

1. With scrap of yarn, using a crochet hook, make chains 5–10 stitches more than the number of cast-on stitches.

2. Lay the chain flat with the bumps facing up, as shown in photo below. Insert a needle under a purl bump.

3. Pick up the number of cast-on stitches.

LOOP STITCH

1. Knit a stitch as usual, but don't take off the stitch on the left needle.
2. Bring the working yarn in front between needles.
3. Wrap your thumb with working yarn from under the thumb to over.
4. Knit a stitch onto the remaining stitch on the left needle.
5. Pass the first knitted stitch over the second stitch to tie a loop.
6. Repeat the loop stitch as many times as the pattern requires.

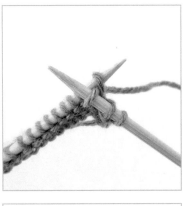

I-CORD

1. Knit stitches on double-point needle normally.

2. Slide the stitches from one end of double-point needle to the other.

3. Without turning double-point needle, place the double-point needle in your left hand.

4. Pull the yarn so that it is snug; then knit stitches from the left to the right double-point needle.